STOCKHOLM

THE CITY AT A GLANCE

Gamla Stan

The maze of cobbled streets and well-preserved old merchants' houses making up this charming island may be well trodden by tourists, but if you're looking to buy a classic reindeer skin or archetypal Swedish cheese slicer, then look no further.

Centralbron

Stockholm's central artery, Centralbron is a railroad and car bridge that runs through the Old Town (Gamla Stan), connecting the main city centre to Södermalm, the trendy, up-and-coming boho district.

Central Station

Not only the main railway link to the suburbs and beyond, Central Station is also the place to catch the Arlanda Express – the city's super-efficient 20-minute connection to the airport.

Riksdagshuset

Little Helgeandsholmen (Isle of the Holy Spirit) is almost completely taken up by the Swedish Parliament. The modern section added in the 1970s (shown in the city view) is a great example of the Swedish finesse at marrying contemporary styles with old.

Drottninggatan

One of the city's main shopping drags, highlights of this pedestrianised street include the old cinema Skandia (converted into a bank) and the restaurant, Grill.
See p041

Kulturhuset

A cultural focal point in Stockholm, with exhibitions, performances and a library. The building also houses a superb art bookstore (Konst-ig) and design store (DesignTorget).
See p012

INTRODUCTION
THE CHANGING FACE OF THE URBAN SCENE

Open to change but always retaining a smattering of Nordic cool, noughties Stockholm is an edgy, flirtatious, party city. The late-1990s trend of sleek white minimalism may have highlighted the capital as a pilgrim site for the design conscious but today the city has reached a new depth that challenges the notion that Stockholm and its inhabitants are 'only' ravishingly beautiful. Even the smart, conservative, groomed central area of Östermalm has opened itself up to cosmopolitan influences. And Södermalm – the island south of Gamla Stan (the Old Town) – has established itself as the young, trendy, boho-chic area with a cultural and commercial value that deserves more than a passing nod.

As well as this shift in focus away from the centre, the city has also altered stylistically. The ubiquitous white tabletops, clean seating areas and tealight ambience has been updated and many commercial interiors have taken on individual, experimental and altogether more fun undertones. The locals themselves, with their well-spoken English, zest for life and love of travelling, have recently taken all these foreign influences to heart. Yet amid all their enthusiasm is a strong sense of self-awareness. Stockholmers have an incredible quality of never taking things too far. Whether it's in design, architecture, fashion or catering, Swedes just seem to achieve the ideal balance. They've even got the perfect word for it, *lagom*, which means 'just right'.

ESSENTIAL INFO
FACTS, FIGURES AND USEFUL ADDRESSES

TOURIST OFFICE
Sverigehuset, Hamngatan 27
T 5082 8508
www.stockholmtown.com

TRANSPORT
Car hire
Avis
T 797 9970
Hertz
T 797 9900
Metro
T 600 1000
www.sl.se/english
Taxis
Taxi Kurir
T 300 000
Taxi Stockholm
T 150 000
Taxi 020
T 020 202 020
www.taxi020.se

EMERGENCY SERVICES
Ambulance (and general emergencies)
T 112
Police (non-emergency)
T 114 14
24-hour pharmacy
Apotek CW Scheele
Klarabergsviadukten 64
T 454 8130

EMBASSIES
British
Skarpögatan 6-8
T 671 3000
www.britishembassy.se
US
Dag Hammarskjölds Väg 31
T 783 5300
stockholm.usembassy.gov

MONEY
American Express
T 429 5600
www10.americanexpress.com

POSTAL SERVICES
Post Office
Centralstationen
T 781 2425
Shipping
UPS
T 020 788 799
www.ups.com

BOOKS
Stockholm: City of My Dreams by Per
Andrews Fogelstrom (Penfield Press)
The Messiah of Stockholm by Cynthia
Ozick (Random House USA)

WEBSITES
Architecture
www.arkitekturmuseet.se
Art
www.modernamuseet.se
Design
www.fargfabriken.se
www.svenskform.se
Newspapers
www.thelocal.se

COST OF LIVING
Taxi from Arlanda Airport to city centre
€41
Cappuccino
€3
Packet of cigarettes
€4.10
Daily newspaper
€1.60
Bottle of champagne
€33.50

STOCKHOLM
Area
188 sq km
Population
760,000
Currency: Swedish krona
SEK1 = £0.07 = €0.11 = $0.13
Telephone codes
Sweden: 46
Stockholm: 8
Time
GMT +1

AVERAGE MAX TEMPERATURE / °C

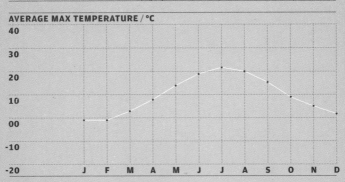

AVERAGE RAINFALL / MM

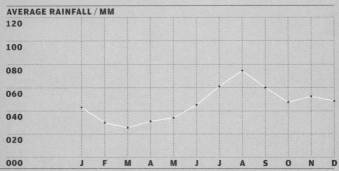

NEIGHBOURHOODS

THE AREAS YOU NEED TO KNOW AND WHY

To help you navigate the city, we've chosen the most interesting districts (see the map inside the back cover) and underlined featured venues in colour, according to their location (see below); those venues that are outside these areas are not coloured.

ÖSTERMALM

With the most prime property in Sweden, manicured boulevards and chic shopping centres, this is the place to check out which labels are in and which are 'so last year'. Filled with yummy mummys, the snazzy media set and plenty of old money, its happy residents rarely go anywhere else.

SKEPPSHOLMEN

Othewise known as Museum Island, this tiny area is to all intents and purposes made up of Svensk Form (Design Museum), Moderna Museet (Modern Art Museum) and Arkitekturmuseet (Architecture Museum). All three are worthy of a visit.

NORRMALM

The bustling city centre Norrmalm is the capital's business hub. Filled with offices, coffee chains and lunch spots, it's not exactly a quaint area, but when it contains Stockholm's largest department store, NK – think the equivalent of Selfridges or Bloomingdales – then who needs cute?

SÖDERMALM

Until ten years ago parts were considered too dangerous to venture into at night (in Swedish terms anyway), but today this trendy, boho part of town tells a different story. Transformed into a creative hub, the area named Sofo (south of Folkungagatan) is littered with cutting-edge boutiques, yoga studios and beatnik cafés. Think skinny jeans and plenty of black thick-rimmed specs.

VASASTAN

This mainly residential district attracts families looking for a bit more space but still wanting the benefits of inner-city life. A few more bars and restaurants have sprung up recently to give the place an increasingly hip vibe, but for the most part this is a local area with neighbourhood eateries and organic delis.

GAMLA STAN

Packed full of character and tourists, the Old Town is the olde worlde part of the city. A maze of cobbled streets and terracotta-coloured buildings, the area is pretty much made up of restaurants, bars and gift shops. Veer away from the main strip, Västerlanggatan, to find some charming antique shops and adorable cafés.

KUNGSHOLMEN

Up-and-coming as a residential area for young creatives who have been pushed out of Östermalm by rocketing rents. The island's huge houses have been converted into loft-living spaces with a few cosy local bistros and small galleries springing up.

DJURGÅRDEN

This lush, green, urban garden is the city's oasis. The area contains the zoo, funfair and several museums, and manages to do so in the least tacky way possible. The route along the water, shaded by the emerald canopy of trees, is definitely up there with the best jogging routes in the world.

LANDMARKS
THE SHAPE OF THE CITY SKYLINE

Alongside the regular collection of painted canvases and framed photographs that line the walls of the <u>Moderna Museet</u> (see p010) are rectangular windows that reveal breathtaking views of Stockholm's harbour. In other words, for the Swedes, a view over the landscape is just as beautiful as any work of art.

Then again, given that the city is built on 14 islands and a series of 24,000 smaller ones in the archipelago beyond, that it casts a striking picture isn't that surprising. Separated only by a short walk across one of 57 bridges, each of the main islands has its own character. Norrmalm has a buzzing, city-centre feel, while Gamla Stan, just a stop away on the subway, is all picturesque cobbled streets and cosy cafés. Östermalm, which is a densely filled residential and shopping area, is very different from lush, green Djurgården, but just a quick skip over Djurgårdsbron.

With the skyline so dominated by the water, landmarks tend to take second place. Kaknästornet (see p013), the telecom building, can be seen from almost anywhere. Newer structures, such as Globen (see p090), which was completed in 1989, and the <u>Moderna Museet</u>, rebuilt between 1995 and 1998, fit very comfortably within Stockholm's panorama, while <u>Kulturhuset</u> (see p012) in Norrmalm, located slap bang in the city centre, is perhaps the ideal landmark from which to navigate.

For all addresses, see Resources.

Moderna Museet

Originally housed in a 19th-century navy drill house, it wasn't until the mid-1990s that the Museum of Modern Art had its striking minimal makeover. Designed by Spanish architect Rafael Moneo in collaboration with White Architects, the museum was forced to close for two years due to problems with damp but emerged triumphant in 2004 with an improved interior, extended permanent collection and no admission fee. Now it stands proud on Skeppsholmen, as loved for its art — the museum houses one of the largest collections of 20th-century works in Europe, plus numerous Swedish and Nordic sculptures, paintings and installations — as its spacious galleries, subtle exterior and outstanding café.
Skeppsholmen, T 5195 5200,
www.modernamuseet.se

Kulturhuset

A counterpoint to the commercialism of the inner-city redevelopment of Hötorget, Peter Celsing's remarkable building at Sergels Torg beat off all other contenders in a 1965 competition. Incorporating two buildings into one – the Kulturhuset (Culture House) and Civic Theatre with the Riksbanken (Bank of Sweden) – was no simple task. Rather than try to unify two such different functions, Celsing did just the opposite. Kulturhuset was given a completely glass-fronted facade that showcases the activities inside while in stark contrast the Bank is a heavy, introverted, black granite cube.

Sergels Torg 3, T 5083 1508,
www.kulturhuset.stockholm.se

Kaknästornet

Known as the central 'spider' in the web of Sweden's TV and radio networks, this imposing 155m-high steel and concrete structure owes little other connection to an arachnid. Drawn up by architects Bengt Lindroos and Hans Borgström, it took four years to build and opened in 1967. Like so many other 1960s buildings, the stark tower has dramatically divided city opinion over the years. Few residents, however, could argue that the view from the top-floor restaurant (which despite a refurb, doesn't quite make the grade in terms of dining) is anything but spectacular. *Mörka Kroken 28-30, T 667 2105, www.kaknastornet.se*

Koppartälten
Built in 1787 by set designer Louis-Jean Desprez for the King's Guardsmen, the three Copper Tents are a magical addition to the already dreamlike Haga Park. The middle tent houses a museum detailing the park's history, while the chic café in the eastern tent, designed by Torbjörn Olsson, is an aluminium masterpiece. *Hagaparken, Solna, T 277 002, www.koppartalten.se*

HOTELS

WHERE TO STAY AND WHICH ROOMS TO BOOK

A few years ago, Stockholm would have struggled to house the visitors to any large event or conference. This is no longer so, thanks largely to the opening of two hotels to the south of the city in 2003 – the mighty Clarion Hotel (see p026), with 532 rooms, and the smaller 99-room Hotel Rival (Mariatorget 3, T 5457 8900). While both were well received, the older hotels have not fallen out of favour, and impeccable service and constant updates have kept the established forefathers on top.

The Grand Hôtel (see p023), which recently renovated its lobby and opened a new bar and restaurant on the ground floor, gained 76 new rooms and suites when it acquired the Burmanska Palace next door in July 2006. At the same time, the Berns Hotel (see p021) gave its Clock Suite an overhaul and is renovating the rest. While none of these hotels could be described as monolithic – save perhaps the Clarion – bizarrely the boutique concept is largely unrepresented. The deliciously hip newcomer Hotel Hellsten (see p030) claims that status on the basis that each room has a different design and furnishings, but it's rather too large at 80 suites. The traditional Hotel Esplanade (see p018) is perhaps the only centrally located qualifier, but for real cosiness, you need to go out of town, where the J Sealodge Gåshaga (see p028) has just 13 modern rooms, with sea views that are unsurpassed.

For all addresses and room rates, see Resources.

Hotel Birger Jarl

Don't get put off by the bland 1970s lobby and exterior. Once past the entrance, this caterpillar of a hotel metamorphoses into a butterfly. Here you will find a myriad of individually styled rooms by top Swedish and international designers. Choose from the Gotland Room (Room 701) by Kristian Eriksson of GAD, the hi-tech boys' room by Love Arbén (Room 708), the polka-dot-clad Mr Glad (Room 705, above) and Miss Dottie (Room 709), both by Thomas Sandell (apparently fought over by Japanese guests) or Jonas Bohlin's Currant Suite (Suite 710), named after the currant bushes that grow on the terrace.

Tulegaten 8, T 674 1800, www.birgerjarl.se

Hotel Esplanade
If you like your hotels to have character,
look no further. The lobby is full of photos
of how the place looked when it opened
in 1910 as Jugend-style apartments, and
the art nouveau flooring, panelling and
fireplaces all remain intact and give it
an old-fashioned Scandinavian charm.
We like Room 10 (pictured).
Strandvägen 7A, T 663 0740,
www.hotelesplanade.se.

Berns Hotel

Traditionally recognised as the hippest and most centrally located hotel in the city, it was the attached chi-chi, celebrity-filled nightclub that made this place's reputation. These days, the Berns may have matured, but there's no sign of its popularity or looks fading – the club has just reopened after a major refit, there's a live music schedule on the bar terrace in summer and a new head chef is kick-starting the kaiseki (a kind of high-end Japanese tapas) restaurant into the top spot. Rooms 606 and 608 have huge terraces for hosting private soirées, while the stunning Clock Suite (above and left), with views from the galleried bedroom overlooking most of Stockholm, must surely be the ideal place to wake up. *Näckströmsgatan 8, T 5663 2200, www.berns.se*

Nordic Light Hotel

A stone's throw from where the Arlanda Express (airport train) drops you off, this sleek, well-designed lobby (above) serving tip-top cocktails certainly makes a good first impression. But the hotel has another trick up its sleeve – mood-altering rooms. Equipped with 60 Superior Mood and Deluxe Mood suites, guests are given a chart explaining how different lighting tones can influence emotion and are encouraged to twiddle with the settings. Admittedly it's a bit gimmicky but as the standard rooms can be pokey, the suites are worth picking for their size if nothing else. The two Deluxe corner rooms are by far the best, while having your breakfast brought up by room service whatever time you happen to wake is a nice bonus. *Vasaplan 7, T 5056 3000, www.nordiclighthotel.se*

Grand Hôtel

Rich, opulent and boasting a guest list that includes most of the royalty, heads of states and superstars ever to visit the city, this is one hotel that lives up to its name. Despite the reputation, the Grand refuses to rest on its laurels. Seventy-six new rooms opened in July 2006 in Burmanska Palace next door, including a new penthouse suite. An exclusive restaurant and renovated caviar bar set the scene in the lobby, while views over the harbour from the south side (even from a double room, above) are simply breathtaking. Should the heavy Gustavian style of the Bernadotte Suite be too much, there are eight charming Junior Suites, one of which, room 150, is done up with Svenskt Tenn furniture and fabrics. *Södra Blasieholmshamnen 8, T 679 3500, www.grandhotel.se*

Hall of Mirrors, Grand Hôtel

Clarion Hotel

A new upstart in the buzzing Södermalm district, at 532 rooms even the Clarion admits that you're not going to feel at home here. Instead the hotel's proprietors will make you 'feel happily curious and refreshed', with which we'd certainly agree. The lobby or Waterfall Lounge (right) with a water feature adjacent to the elevators sets the tone, while rooms, such as the standard double (above), are light, comfortable and user-friendly. On the top floor, the hot tub and sauna that overlook a busy motorway stretch are a real highlight. If you find the two-floored Söder Suite, complete with open fire and round hot tub, is occupied, ask for the south-facing Penthouse Suite. And we challenge you to think of anything they might have missed out in the sumptuous smorgasbord that is the breakfast buffet.
Ringvägen 98, T 462 1000,
www.clarionstockholm.com

J Sealodge Gåshaga
Situated 15 minutes by car or 30 by train or boat from the city centre, the hotel has only 13 rooms, each with a balcony and sea view. The decor was inspired by a summer house in Newport, USA, and the open fires and thick blankets may well make you feel like you're in a Ralph Lauren advert. Not such a bad thing.
Värdshusvägen 14-16, Lidingö, T 601 3410, www.restaurantj.com

Hotel Hellsten

Short of renting an apartment, Hotel Hellsten might be the closest you're going to get to feeling like you're actually living in the city. Designed in the old style of the typical bourgeois Stockholm flats, complete with wooden panels and 'kakelugn' – charming tile or porcelain stoves characteristic of Sweden – the Hellsten, which opened in late 2005, is the most recent addition to the city's hotel scene. Design and furnishings are different in all 80 rooms, but they centre around a swanky, minimal and utterly charming theme, and are filled with antiques collected by owner Per Hellsten from Asia, Europe and Sweden. The four-poster bed in Suite 1201 is a treat while the red walls, elaborate panelling and crystal chandelier in Room 1302 (right) will make you wish you really did live here.
Luntmakargatan 68, T 661 8600, www.hellsten.se

24 HOURS

SEE THE BEST OF THE CITY IN JUST ONE DAY

Stockholm is a city of climatic contrast, with temperatures falling to -10°C in the winter months and climbing to a bright 25°C with close to 24 hours of daylight in the summer, rendering a complete transformation. Equally notable is the city's ability to go from tranquil, bucolic landscape to bustling shopping district in only a few minutes. These extremes unite rather than divide the city, as Stockholmers embrace their separate seasons with gusto.

Regardless of the season, a visit to the pretty, peaceful island of Djurgården can't fail to put you in a good mood. The winding path leading right by the water's edge is one of the best jogging routes in the world, while a half-hour stroll through the woods is a glorious start to any day. Swedish breakfast is also a divine experience to be savoured. While pickled fish, strong cheese and crackerbread continue to divide foreigners' tastes, the speciality bread and pastries always go down well. A full stomach allows you to tackle Östermalm where, concentrated within a tiny area, are some of Europe's finest design showrooms and boutiques.

Gamla Stan (Old Town) may be a tourist trap but its magical appeal – not to mention the snug atmosphere at Kaffekoppen (see p037) – means it shouldn't be missed. For a laid-back dinner, the buzzy, candlelit ambience at Bakfickan (see p038) is our choice, followed by late-night cocktails on the terrace at Nox (see p039). *For all addresses, see Resources.*

09.00 Djurgården

Djurgården is one of the 14 islands that make up Stockholm city, but that's as far as its association with the word city goes. A lushly wooded park, lined with shaded walkways, grassy knolls and waterside pathways, a light jog or stroll under the emerald green canopy of Djurgården's trees (and should the weather allow, a quick dip in the water) is the ideal way to start the day. Located amid this parkland is the zoo, tivoli, circus, museums and various restaurants (summer dining at Lisa På Udden, Biskopsvägen 7, T 660 9475 is unsurpassed).

11.00 Brunch

After all that morning air, you'll no doubt be in need of sustenance. Locals credit Riddarbageriet as serving the best latte in town, while the bread and pastries, made fresh throughout the day by award-winning master baker Johan Sörberg, are true flour power. For a more substantial feed, the brunch buffet on the Veranda (terrace) at the Grand Hôtel (see p023) is a veritable institution. We recommend you eat Scandi-style with herring, gravadlax and sliced cheese piled high on cracker bread. Alternatively, it does a great line in scrambled eggs, bacon and pancakes.
Riddargatan 15, T 660 3375

14.00 Shopping

Stockholm's vast landscape is strewn with some of the finest retail wonders in Europe. Start at the distinctive Svenskt Tenn (above, see p073) and continue walking to Gamla Lampor (see p076) on Nybrogatan, where fine vintage lamps looking for good homes blanket the walls and ceilings. Carry on to Östermalmstorg and you will find Modernity (see p074), a treasure trove of Scandinavian vintage furniture and glassware. Asplund (see p078), further up Sibyllegatan, houses the best in Swedish contemporary design, while Jacksons (see p084) – a couple of blocks up – will tempt even the most hardened maximalist to embrace vintage Scandinavian.

16.00 Kaffekoppen

Just across the bridge is Gamla Stan. The island may be the most tourist-heavy area of Stockholm but with good reason. The narrow cobblestone alleys and classic buildings on either side are enchanting and become even more so when sprinkled with a covering of snow in the winter months. A short stroll is all you need to soak up the atmosphere, but a quick pop into the Nobel Museum (Börshuset, Stortorget, T 5348 1800) on the main square will satisfy any culture cravings. Just opposite, the snug, candlelit café Kaffekoppen serves a divine hot chocolate in oversized mugs, while the apple cake with custard is total perfection.
Stortorget 20, T 203 170

19.30 Bakfickan

A low-lit, informal counter restaurant, Bakfickan (or 'Hip Pocket', which is the rather unfortunate translation) is a popular eaterie with simple yet superb food. If you want a more sumptuous dining experience, Operakällaren next door (see p058) is your place but with its dark green lampshades, white tiles, chalkboard menu and friendly, laid-back atmosphere, this is a well-cushioned and relaxing end to the perfect day. You can't reserve a table, and the place does get pretty rammed on weekends, but it does serve until 11.30pm. Plenty of time then to sip on a cold beer, before sitting down to some lavish Swedish treats that include herring with egg, chives and sour cream and grilled scallops with bleak roe. *Jakobs Torg 12, Operahuset, Kungsträdgarden, T 676 5809*

21.00 Nox

Smoker or not, this is the kind of terrace that everyone can appreciate. Located out back so you don't have to deal with passers-by, and filled with plants, mood lighting and outdoor pouffes to lounge on, this is one beer garden that Nox out the competition. And the inside's not bad either, complete with black walls, black leather sofas and a vibrant, illuminated green bar. Opened in 2005, the venue (along with the well-priced restaurant downstairs) has quickly climbed the ranks to attract a design-savvy, well-dressed crowd until 1am most nights of the week. *Grev Turegatan 30, T 5458 2400, www.nox.se*

URBAN LIFE
CAFÉS, RESTAURANTS, BARS AND NIGHTCLUBS

There is a theory that Swedes hanker after great interior design because they have dinner parties rather than go out. This is easily disproved by a night on the tiles in the capital. Aside from perhaps Sundays when many of the restaurants are closed, Stockholm's eateries are always packed (booking is essential on Fridays and Saturdays). True, it's not cheap and the infamous Scandinavian alcohol prices are scary, but in return the quality is outstanding. Food is fresh, menus are very exciting and most of the high-end restaurants have wine cellars to rival the finest establishments in New York and Paris. Competition between nightspots is fierce with hot new venues opening up all the time.

What hasn't changed is the Swedish love affair for a coffee, cake and a good gossip. The notion of *fika* ('to have coffee'), along with Stockholm's prowess at keeping the corporate coffeehouse chains off the high streets, has created a vibrant café culture.

For nightlife, however, Stockholm is fairly conservative during the week. Bars are open daily, usually until midnight or 1am, but tend to stay quiet until Thursday, Friday and Saturday when the party goes on well into the early hours and queuing is routine. It's also worth being aware of the differing dress codes across the city – from the smart suited-and-booted style in the bars in Östermalm to the vintage, dress-down look in Södermalm.

For all addresses, see Resources.

Grill

Located in a furniture showroom, this large, informal and vibrant restaurant combines crystal chandeliers and velvet wallpaper with sleek, white minimalism. Designed in partnership with Swedish furniture manufacturer Fogia, the idea was to create different rooms all in one space, giving the sense that this is a meeting place rather than a restaurant. The result is a mishmash of styles that manages to avoid looking contrived. The food is equally exceptional without being pretentious, with a menu that stretches from burger with foie gras, apple and truffle crème to ribs of deer (all grilled in one of five different styles: brick oven, rotisserie, smoke, charcoal or table grill). *Drottninggatan 89, T 314 530, www.grill.se*

Viola
The party hot spot in Östermalm, Viola is all spangly chandeliers, white leather booths, painted Laura Ashley-relief wallpaper and exquisite cocktails, which combine to make this camp palace of fun the best bar in town for mixing with the catwalk set – you might even spot princesses Madeleine and Victoria.
Humlegårdsgatan 14, T 664 5535, www.sthlmsfinest.se

Edsbacka Krog

It may be a 20-minute taxi ride out of town, but if the two Michelin stars aren't enough to tempt you, then the historic, thick-walled building dating back to 1626 and steeped in history will. Reminiscent of a dilapidated country inn, in the most positive sense, open fireplaces and low-hanging beams make the decor as reassuring and soothing as the menu. Don't miss out on head chef and owner Christer Lindström's famed saddle of roe deer with blackcurrant sauce – good enough to make you weep. For gastronomic experiences, this is quite simply the best in Stockholm. *Sollentunavägen 220, T 963 300, www.edsbackakrog.se*

Esperanto

Opened in November 2005, Esperanto's simple, no-frills concept of good food, good venue and good service is starting to catch on with locals. Determined not to be placed in any category, be it Swedish, Italian, French, etc, the owners chose the name of the establishment on the basis that food is an international language. The menu is therefore based on which ingredients go best together and, to keep it simple, there are only two choices you have to make – four courses or seven. Dishes are small but perfectly formed, with past delights including the delectable pigeon 'ras-el-hanout' and melt-in-your-mouth whipped brie with truffle bread, while the carefully chosen wine menu offers a different grape to go with each course. *Kungstensgatan 2, T 696 2323, www.esperantorestaurant.se*

Allmänna Galleriet 925
On the first floor of an unimposing office
building, this loft-style restaurant and
bar is owned by Englishman Joe Black,
hence the shabby-chic Shoreditch vibe.
Ease into a Chesterfield, admire the
Jonas Bohlin furniture and Tom Dixon
lights and take comfort in the knowledge
that you're hanging with the in-crowd.
*Kronobergsgatan 37, T 4106 8100,
www.ag925.se*

Locanda Klara Norra

This lunch spot may be rather smart if you're just after a quick refuel, but if you'd rather rest those weary shopping legs for a little longer, then pull up a pew. A popular place for a business lunch – we're talking creative media types, so don't worry about not being suited up – Locanda is a buzzing daytime restaurant and café that becomes somewhat more subdued come dinner. The Southern European-inspired food is hearty and good, served in portions that are enough to satisfy but not make you drowsy, and along with a fine wine list, there's also 20 different types of mineral water to try. *Mäster Samuelsgatan 60, T 440 2380, www.locanda.se*

Teatergrillen

This no-windows restaurant, complete with low lighting, red velvet booths and stone walls, comes as close to power dining, mafia-style, as it gets in Sweden. Taking full advantage of its proximity to Dramaten (the magnificent theatre founded by King Gustav III in 1788 for Swedish dramas to be performed in their original language), the interior takes on a luxurious *Moulin Rouge* feel, with a collection of masks and costumes and a frieze depicting a stunning view over the rooftops of Paris. Ask for the corner booth (table 53), order the salt-baked entrecôte with béarnaise, warm horseradish and pommes Pont Neuf, then head to aristocratic members' club Noppe's Bar next door to clinch the deal. *Nybrogatan 3, T 5450 3565, www.teatergrillen.se*

Marie Laveau
Named after the voodoo queen of New
Orleans, this bar, restaurant and newly
added nightclub is where the groovy,
vintage-clad Södermalm crowd hang
out after dark. Bands and DJs play
the sweaty basement, while food and
drinks are served upstairs. The club's
open until 3am Wednesday to Saturday.
Hornsgatan 66, T 668 8500,
www.marielaveau.se

Fredsgatan 12

Referred to by locals as F12, this place is number one for sampling modern Swedish cooking at its best. A complete makeover courtesy of Lomar Arkitekter in 2003 had the place decked out with B&B furniture, lighting by Moooi and Kartell and the finest in contemporary art, courtesy of the Wetterling Gallery, all of which means that today F12 is a restaurant you won't get anywhere near unless you book ahead.

For something a little less formal, try the sister restaurant Kungsholmen: the place is based on a food court, with six different stations offering high-quality food in a rather relaxed and anything-goes setting.
Fredsgatan 12, T 248 052, www.f12.se

Lux

Formerly the canteen for workers in the neighbouring Electrolux factory, following a dramatic renovation in 2003 the name Lux stands more for luxury than Electrolux. A huge listed brick building beautifully set on the island of Lilla Essingen, this is a taxi ride out of town but if you have the time, the food and calm ambience of Lux are worth it – especially for the six weeks in the summer when dinner is served on the veranda. Menu-wise, don't leave here without trying the grilled cheek of cod, while for the sweet-toothed there's a wide selection of puddings and specially made chocolates squealing for your attention.
Primusgatan 116, T 619 0190,
www.luxstockholm.com

Haga Forum

Winter brunch is best at Haga Forum
(a short taxi ride from the city centre).
An odd, unbecoming exterior gives away
the building's previous incarnation as
a bus terminal, yet a chalet-like interior
complete with roaring fire and modern
furniture more than makes up for it.
Popular for business lunches during
the week, it is at the weekend when
the place comes into its own, with the
brunch buffet served between noon
and 4pm. We'd recommend you pile
your plate high with the Scando treats
of herrings, prawns and gravadlax,
but should you still have room, or just
can't resist another course, there are
ribs, hamburgers, chicken dishes, salads
and a decadent dessert table to tempt
you. And to walk it off, the vast, magical
landscape of Haga Park lies just outside.
Annerovägen 4, Solna, T 334 844,
http://hagaforum.gastrogate.com

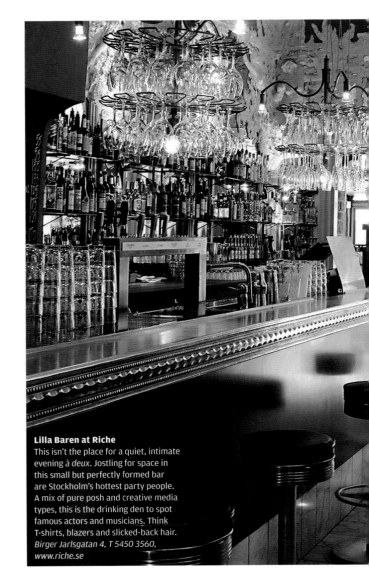

Lilla Baren at Riche
This isn't the place for a quiet, intimate evening *à deux*. Jostling for space in this small but perfectly formed bar are Stockholm's hottest party people. A mix of pure posh and creative media types, this is the drinking den to spot famous actors and musicians. Think T-shirts, blazers and slicked-back hair.
Birger Jarlsgatan 4, T 5450 3560,
www.riche.se

Operakällaren

The direct translation may be 'opera cellar' but this is no dingy basement. Set on the ground floor with views over the water to the palace, the dining room is nothing short of a fairytale. In late 2005 the place was given a facelift by darlings of the local architecture world Claesson, Koivisto Rune who, while praised for their clever use of huge golden mirrors to make full use of the exquisite ceiling and stunning chandeliers, have come in for criticism with their upholstered chairs and lights. Love it or loathe it, the refurb has brought the place back onto the A-list and while you're bound to find the odd tourist within its carved oak walls, this is no reason to miss out on the place that (still) makes the locals most proud.
Operahuset, Karl X11:s Torg, T 676 5801, www.operakallaren.se

The White Room

Open only on Fridays and Saturdays, this minimally designed bar gets all the interior oomph it needs from the dandy boys and sparkly girls inside. Kicking off well after midnight, it might be an undignified scramble to get in, but queuing up is all part and parcel of the party experience in Stockholm. An open-plan layout and pumping music means that conversation is eschewed in favour of posing and dancing, however, as is the case with most happening bars and clubs in Stockholm these days. The all-important deals and chat happen in the tiny cornered-off area on the pavement outside – whether you're a smoker or not.
Regeringsgatan 61, T 5450 7665, www.whiteroom.se

Centro
With its moody ambience, black leather
seating, nouvelle cuisine menu and
(it has to be said) extortionate prices,
this super-slick restaurant and bar is
a reminder of the 1980s glory days.
The bar is the main highlight here
(as are the ethereal toilets) with local
DJs playing to a sparkly party crowd.
*Regeringsgatan 66, T 233 400,
www.centro.nu*

INSIDER'S GUIDE
VIKTORIA HAMBERGER, CREATIVE DIRECTOR

Our Stockholm girl-about-town works for Brindfors Enterprise, Sweden's largest graphic design company, whose clients include Absolut Vodka, Arla Foods and Electrolux. Living in Östermalm, Hamberger recommends Divino as a good local lunch stop for tasty pasta dishes and fresh salads, while for something sweeter, Saturnus Café, just down the road, has excellent cakes. For brunch her favourite haunt is Haga Forum (see p054): 'A beautiful setting for champagne, prawn cocktails and other treats.' Working lunch is best in the buzzing atmosphere at Grill (see p041).

Mrs H, home to labels such as Sonia Rykiel, Eley Kishimoto and Seven, is a favourite shopping haunt. Skin Deep is ideal for jeans, and fashion designer Whyred heads the homegrown talent. In Södermalm, C/O Stockholm has excellent make-up and skin creams as well as fab shoes, handbags and accessories. For furniture, Deco Design is crammed with bargains, Asplund (see p078) is best for modern design while Svenskt Tenn (see p073) 'may not be cheap but it is having something of a renaissance'. Nitty Gritty does clothes, books, records, shoes et al.

For casual dinners, Sabai-Soong serves great Thai food, while Roppongi has unbeatable sushi. For drinks after work, Allmänna Galleriet 925 (see p046) is a relaxed, easy-going place, and for a night of music and hanging out with friends, the Riche restaurant and bar (see p056) is an old favourite that is 'still going strong'.

ARCHITOUR
A GUIDE TO STOCKHOLM'S ICONIC BUILDINGS

When the Social Democratic Party implemented its progressive reforms in 1932, public housing projects were highlighted as Swedish architecture's main task. Stockholm's landscape waved goodbye to the elaborate neo-classical buildings made popular at the turn of the century by architects such as Ivar Tengbom and Erik Gunnar Asplund in favour of stern, modern projects that embraced a functionalist aesthetic. A strict government agenda meant that gaining planning permission for individuals became near impossible, and with ambitious projects such as the Million Homes Program between 1965 and 1975, few architects were given much scope to experiment and shine, with the exception of Celsing's super-modern structure Kulturhuset (see p012) of 1974.

Aside from a brief building boom in the late 1980s that saw private developers take a leading role, it wasn't until the mid-1990s that new and intriguing modern structures started to crop up. The change may be slow but it is definitely steady. The rapid growth of the IT industry generated demand for new office space and with several young and interesting architecture practices set up in the city (for example White Architects and Sandellsandberg) as well as a keen interest to get foreign architects (such as Foster and Partners) involved in shaping the landscape, Stockholm is starting to gain the forward-thinking landmarks it deserves.

For all addresses, see Resources.

Stadsbiblioteket

Erik Gunnar Asplund's last building to embrace Nordic classicism, Stockholm's public library is perhaps the capital's most internationally acclaimed building. Designed after a trip to the United States in 1924, the inspiration was a temple of wisdom, borrowing forms and ornament from ancient Egypt. A processional path from the entrance leads you up the stairs into the magnificent broad cylindrical sphere. Various different reading rooms and administrative areas line the perimeter while the lending hall, the library's heart, is a breathtaking panorama of books with unique architectural detailing that makes this building a photographer's dream.
Sveavägen 73, T 5083 1100, www.ssb.stockholm.se

Lending Hall, Stadsbiblioteket

Gåshaga Brygga
This exclusive residential complex on the island of Lidingö set new standards for affluent living standards when it opened in 2001. Designed by architect Thomas Sandell in conjunction with NCC, it is made up of 40 elegant two and three-storey houses, some with cantilevered sections over the water. Plain concrete exteriors reveal stunning, individually designed minimal interiors complete with large windows, spacious terraces, open layouts and private mooring points. Unusually, the development evolved from landowners and not the municipality. With wonderful views and a calm, relaxed atmosphere, these units are among the most extravagant of the city's recent housing projects.
Gåshaga Brygga 13, T 282 828

Millesgården

The former home and studio of sculptor Carl Milles (1875-1955) may be firmly embedded on the tourist trail but don't let that put you off. A stunning sculpture park designed with terraces, fountains, stairways, columns and immense views across the waters of Värtan, this is just one of those places that gets everyone's approval. Add to this the art gallery, which is one of the finest examples of modern architecture latching onto old, and you realise why it's worth ignoring the coaches outside. Designed by J Celsing, modern walls attach to pre-existing stone ones while a huge canopy roof extends over a collection of 17th-century columns. Inside, a generous staircase, white walls, lye-treated fir floors and huge skylights make this gallery a work of art in itself.
Herserudsvägen 32, Lidingö

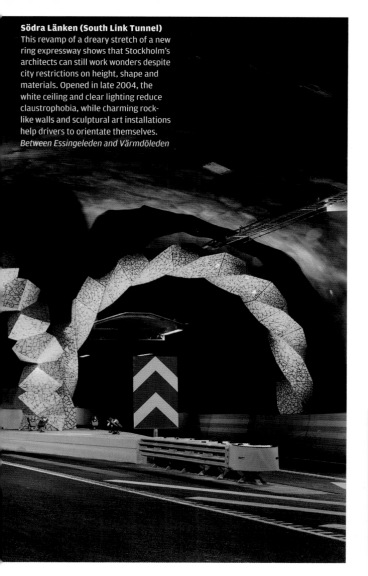

Södra Länken (South Link Tunnel)
This revamp of a dreary stretch of a new
ring expressway shows that Stockholm's
architects can still work wonders despite
city restrictions on height, shape and
materials. Opened in late 2004, the
white ceiling and clear lighting reduce
claustrophobia, while charming rock-
like walls and sculptural art installations
help drivers to orientate themselves.
Between Essingeleden and Värmdöleden

SHOPPING
THE CITY'S BEST SHOPS AND WHAT TO BUY

Scandinavian design has undergone something of a renaissance in the last couple of years, with Sweden as the major player. At least four coffee table books dedicated to the style were published in 2005 alone – *Swedish Design* (Mitchell Beazley), *Scandinavian Design* (Taschen), *Scandinavian Modern* (Ryland Peters & Small) and *Scandinavian Style* (Octopus). Be it established contemporary names such as CKR, Thomas Sandell and Jonas Bohlin, classics from favourites like Josef Frank, Bruno Mathsson and Erik Gunnar Asplund or fresh innovative products by David & Martin, Monica Förster and Anna Kraitz, all are available here in Stockholm. And, unlike many other cities, most of the top design showrooms are within walking distance of each other.

Swedish fashion may be less renowned, but when it comes to original, wearable, high-quality clothes, the Stockholm high street is hard to beat. Brands like Acne and Filippa K are making their mark internationally but are cheaper when buying in Swedish kronor. Less well-known abroad but equally hot locally is preppy Whyred, while newcomer Fifth Avenue Shoe Repair's outlet in Södermalm is one to watch. Nitty Gritty, Mrs H and Riddargatan 12 stock mainly perennial global favourites, such as Sonia Rykiel, Marni and APC, but the collections are always superbly edited and tastefully displayed in fanciful and fresh interiors.

For all addresses, see Resources.

Svenskt Tenn

Despite the recent opening of Svenskt Tenn shop-in-shops in London and New York, they will never be the same as a trip to its flagship Strandvägen boutique. Set up in 1924 by Josef Frank and Estrid Ericson, Svenskt Tenn is an idea, a lifestyle – perhaps even a distinct culture in its own right. Keen to preserve its legacy, the directors are reissuing new pieces and textiles from Frank's archives every year as well as keeping the spirit of Estrid alive in the imaginative window displays and decor. That said, contemporary talents are very much involved in today's new collections, and the store continually buys in pieces from Scandinavian designers, such as this funky candelabra (SEK1,850) by Matti Klenell and Peter Andersson. *Strandvägen 5, T 670 1600, www.svensktienn.se*

Modernity

Originally in Gamla Stan, Modernity moved to this spacious central location in April 2003. Since then the showroom has gone from strength to strength, largely due to the good taste and passion of its owner — not a Swede, but the Scotsman Andrew Duncanson. Famed the world over for its fine vintage collection, particularly by the grand masters of the Scandinavian style, such as Wegner, Mathsson, Aalto, Juhl, Jacobsen, Wirkkala and Sarpaneva, it is the occasional limited editions by various established Swedish designers like Mats Theselius and Jonas Bohlin that are really worth fighting over. In addition, Duncanson's charming way of cunningly sliding in work by his favourite emerging contemporary designers, such as Caroline Schlyter, makes Modernity a must for any design junkie in need of a serious fix. *Sibyllegatan 6, T 208 025, www.modernity.se*

Gamla Lampor
Translated as 'Old Lamps', this shop does exactly what it says on the tin. Charming and unpretentious, there are so many lights here they spill onto the pavement. Whether you're after a floor, table, wall or pendant lamp, you can pick up a vintage piece (the place specialises in 1930s to 1970s) for up to a third less than outside Scandinavia. *Nybrogatan 3, T 611 9035, www.gamlalampor.com*

Asplund

Brothers Michael and Thomas Asplund have been supplying stylish Stockholmers with clean, elegant furniture for over two decades. Stocking both contemporary classics as well as their own commissions from Sweden's top creatives, Asplund has launched several careers, including those of Ola Wihlborg and Stina Sandwall, and has also produced new ranges by old favourites like Claesson Koivisto Rune and Thomas Sandell. Having skirted around the experimental and conceptual aspects of modern Swedish design, the collection remains a testament to elegant, high-quality and functional Scandinavian style.
Sibyllegatan 31, T 662 5284,
www.asplund.org

Schnapps

You can't go to Sweden and not partake in the local schnapps culture. Each region has its own brew and the taste varies according to different distillation processes, flavours and spices. The taste is an acquired one, and it may take a while to establish your preference. Which is why this starter pack by Reimersholms from Systembolaget (200kr), featuring the most popular 10, is ideal to help you refine your palate and pick out those subtle flavours that are tucked behind this 40 per cent proof tipple. Plus, buying alcohol in Sweden from the highly regulated, state-owned Systembolaget is an experience in itself. *www.systembolaget.se*

Konsthantverket

After 55 years at its previous premises,
Konsthantverkarna's boutique moved
to its trendy new location by Slussen in
late 2005 and with it has taken on a
savvy new persona. A kind of union for
professional Swedish craftsmen working
in glass, sculpture, ceramics, textiles,
jewellery, silver, wood and leather, the 166
artists that make up Konsthantverkarna
have cast off old-fashioned handiwork in
favour of slick, high-quality design. With
the shop filled to the brim with table-top
pieces and utensils as well as exclusive
objets d'art, jewellery and ceramics, this
is as much a gallery to go to for inspiration
as it is a shop. That said, everything has
its price (these craftsmen are crafty in
every sense of the word) and once you see
how beautifully the staff wrap the pieces,
we challenge you to leave empty-handed.
Södermalmstorg 4, T 611 0370,
www.konsthantverkana.se

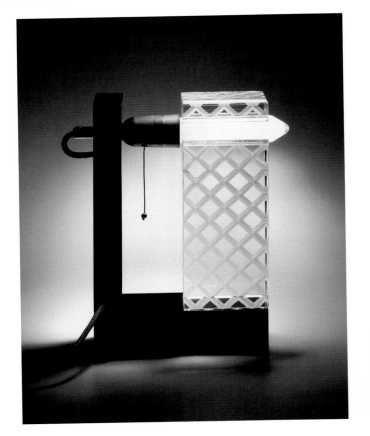

Orrefors/Kosta Boda

With its recent refurb, this Orrefors/Kosta Boda shop just got even crisper. Don't be put off by the tourist influx that tends to crowd into the shop, the two new glass collections launched every year keep the brand vital. Manufactured in four factories situated in Småland, south Sweden, this is quality glassware in a class of its own. However, it is the art glass that sets this company apart. Divided into two groups: Unique, of which only one copy is made; and Limited, of which there are only 60 or less, the products can be anything from functional objects to more sculptural designed pieces. If the swirly patterns and heavy crystal constructions are not to your taste, check out Per B Sundberg's bold and masculine 'Lamp' series instead. *Birger Jarlsgatan 15, T 5450 4084, www.kostaboda.se*

10 Swedish Designers

Formed in 1970, only three of the original 10 Swedish Designers remain but the brand is still creating its trademark bright and bold patterned fabrics. With a large fan base, including fashion tycoon Paul Smith, the products are available in select stores across the globe but there is something very special about seeing the whole collection together in all its brash and audacious glory. With an archive that holds over 700 patterns for fabrics and vinyl cloths and an ever-expanding range that even includes ironing-board covers, this is a great place to pick up gifts, such as this toiletry bag (SEK290) by Tom Hedquist, both for yourself and others. *Götgatan 25, T 643 2504, www.tiogruppen.com*

Jacksons

Whether you're after vintage Artek chairs, rare Svenkst Tenn lighting or some fine antique Murano glass, the self-taught Paul Jackson somehow gets it right every time. This treasure trove of a store opened in Östermalm in 2002, the original gallery in Gamla Stan having been a Stockholm institution since its inception as a small store over 25 years ago. Furniture, glass, ceramics, jewellery, lighting and textiles from the 20th century are sourced from private dealers across the world with an emphasis on Scandinavian furniture and Italian glass. Jacksons claims that 'the carefully vetted selections on display clearly elevate the 20th-century era as one of the most vibrant in the history of creative production'. Work hours are mainly Monday to Friday, as the shop is only open from noon to 3pm on Saturday. *Sibyllegatan 53, T 665 3350, www.jacksons.se*

Apparat

Set up back in 2002 by Nadia Tolstoy and Fredrik Moselius after graduating from Central Saint Martins in London, Apparat is an Aladdin's cave of great design and good ideas. Crammed full of furniture, lighting and stationery, it is the gimmicks and innovative playthings that set this gem of a mini-shop apart (or should we say Apparat?). From the little brass feet that you insert into your soap so you don't get a mucky sink to the sparklers in all the letters of the alphabet, Apparat is full of things that will always prompt others to ask, 'Where did you get that from?'
Nytorgsgatan 36, T 653 6633, www.apparat.nu

Grebbestads Ansjovis Original

Milder than their Italian cousins, Swedish anchovies are delicious to cook with and an essential ingredient in the luscious local casserole dish Jansson's Frestelse. An age-old recipe, Grebbestads' secret blend (SEK27) is rumoured to contain cinnamon and ginger, which gives the anchovies their special tang and makes them an excellent accompaniment to egg sandwiches, trust us. All these reasons, plus the fact that they are sold in their original old-school pink tin dating back to 1911, makes them a worthy souvenir. *Abba Seafood, from good Stockholm supermarkets, www.abba.se*

SPORTS AND SPAS
WORK OUT, CHILL OUT OR JUST WATCH

Considering its small population, Sweden has achieved remarkable success in global sports. Fields like tennis, skiing, golf, athletics and ice hockey regularly produce world champions. In part, this is due to the nation's enthusiasm for keeping fit. Stockholm offers fantastic indoor facilities – such as the dreamy Sturebadet gym, pool and health centre (opposite), 16 indoor courts at Kungliga Tennishallen, and Centralbadet, which puts most other city pools to shame. And with a winter landscape that offers long-distance ice-skating, cross-country skiing, ice hockey and ice fishing just a 10-minute drive from the centre, locals would never let the cold get in the way of staying active. As the old Scandic saying goes: 'There's no such thing as bad weather, just bad clothes.'

Come summer, however, and the Swedes' dedication to staying outside and enjoying the few weeks of glorious sunshine means a great plethora of al fresco activities. Every Stockholmer has their personal favourite bathing spot – be it the large Fågelöudde beach on Lidingö complete with water slides, diving boards and saunas or a hidden little rock on Kastellholmen. The city's proximity to the wet stuff also means that watersports are very popular, with fishing and sailing high on the summer agenda. On land, bicycles are the preferred mode of transport and cyclists are well catered for with specialist lanes and parking bays in abundance.

For all addresses, see Resources.

Sturebadet

A gym, swimming pool and spa founded in 1855 by Carl Curman, this health centre is so cloaked in luxury you'd be forgiven for questioning whether it can actually be good for you. Always quiet, Sturebadet is primarily a members-only club, although it has recently introduced day guest passes (albeit strictly controlled). With over 50 treatments to indulge in, this is the place to have that ultimate Swedish massage, while the Arctic spa treatment that involves stone therapy and a massage with Arctic birch body oil is equally impressive. As former visitors include everyone from the late Greta Garbo to Freddie Ljungberg, this is a great place to spot the rich and famous – with extra marks for catching them in the nuddy. *Sturegallerian 36, T 5450 1500, www.sturebadet.se*

Globen Arena
Still the largest spherical building in the world since its opening in 1989, Sweden's main sporting venue holds 16,000 fans. Known by locals as the giant golfball, the arena is mainly used for ice hockey and innebandy (or floorball as the sport is known internationally). Both are great spectator sports and worth seeing live.
Globentorget 2, T 771 310 000,
www.globearenas.se

Yasuragi Spa
Admittedly the coaches in the car park
might be a turn-off, but this Japanese-
inspired spa is popular for good reason.
With changing rooms you can get lost in,
a large indoor pool, inside and outdoor
Jacuzzis, treatments galore and classes
in everything from meditation to sushi-
making, there's something for everyone.
*Hasseludden, Hamndalsvägen 6, Saltsjö-
Boo, T 747 6100, www.yasuragi.se*

Yachting

If you're looking to spend some time in the archipelago, there's one way to really do it in style – and that's to charter a Swan yacht. Hoist up those sails (or rather let someone else do it for you), feel the wind in your hair, pretend you're in a toothpaste/aftershave advert and kick back watching some of the most idyllic scenery in the world. Yacht Concept has a fleet of over 20 boats to choose from with sizes ranging from 48 foot to the wapping 112-foot super-yacht – which would impress even the likes of Roman Abramovich. Depending on how much time you can spare, boats are available for half a day (six hours), a full day, 24 hours or a week's tour and come equipped with a captain, life jackets, wetsuits and towels. Match with a Henri-Lloyd jacket, Gucci shades and a sunny day for full effect.
Yacht Concept, Grand Hotel Saltsjöbaden, T 717 3650, www.yachtconcept.se

ESCAPES
WHERE TO GO IF YOU WANT TO LEAVE TOWN

For all of Stockholm's attempts to come across as metropolitan, you just know she's a country girl at heart. The city's in such easy reach of so many places of pristine natural beauty that it seems criminal not to take advantage. Most unique and spectacular is the vast, fan-shaped archipelago that stretches out more than 100km from Saltsjön into a magical island world. Known as the 'urban wilderness', the area consists of more than 24,000 islands of which only about a thousand are inhabited. A boater's paradise, with speedboats and yachts for rent (see p094), this span of water is also easily accessed by the several ferries that depart regularly from central Stockholm. Whether you're after a short day trip or a couple of nights' break, the archipelago offers a wide selection of some of the best hotels and restaurants in Scandinavia.

While some larger establishments are open all the year round, most, like Oaxen Skägårdskrog (see p101) and Sands Hotell, tend to be limited to the summer. Because of daylight and temperature reasons, early May to the end of August are the peak times to head out to the archipelago, but winter can offer just as spectacular scenery, with ice-skating and warming up in front of cosy fireplaces being high on the agenda. Alternatively, if you're after something more extreme, the north of Sweden has some of the most challenging and well-maintained ski slopes in Europe.

For all addresses, see Resources.

Grythyttans Gastgivaregard

For those looking for something a little less well-known than the archipelago there is a simple solution: head in the other direction – inland. A two to three-hour drive from Stockholm through pretty spruce forest, tranquil lakes and craggy hillsides and you arrive at the stunning little village of Grythyttan (see p098). Among the old cottages lies a venerable inn with a glorious tongue-twister of a name, Grythyttans Gastgivaregard. Dating from 1640, the building has been lovingly restored into a hotel with over 50 rooms while the restaurant is today a veritable 'temple of gastronomy'. Special weekend rates include accommodation and meals.
Prästgatan 2, T 059 163 300,
www.grythyttan.com

Grythyttan

Åre

Out of all of Sweden's ski resorts in the north of the country, Åre (pronounced awe-re) is the sophisticated choice. Come peak season (December to April) and the slopes and after-ski bars and cafés are filled with the incredibly fresh-faced, healthy-looking Swedish glitterati. Some call it the St Moritz of the north but this may be misleading. Because for all its superb eateries (try the delicious Marmite, Årevägen 72, T 064 750 240, www.marmite.se) and luxury places to stay (Hotel Diplomat Åregården, T 0647 1800, www.diplomathotel.com), Åre is a cosy, charming, gloriously laid-back town. *Tourist info, T 064 717 720, www.are.se*

Oaxen Skägårdskrog

Picturesque without a hint of shabby chic, this is one of the best restaurants in the archipelago. Refreshingly void of tourists, perhaps scared off by its unpronounceable name, this is a waterside eaterie that manages to be romantic and charming without getting lost in wooden-beam, checked-curtain territory. Equally well-balanced between cosy traditional and slick modern is the food cooked by award-winning chef Magnus Ek. An extensive wine list is way beyond standard country fare and if you overdo it on the homemade honey schnapps (and we recommend you do), book one of the five cabins aboard the stunning 1870 yacht (overleaf), which is docked at the mooring point outside. *Hölö, T 5515 3105, www.oaxenkrog.se*

Yacht Hotel, Oaxen Skärgårdskrog

NOTES
SKETCHES AND MEMOS

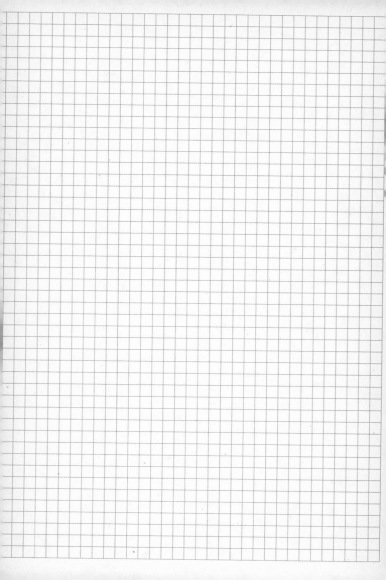

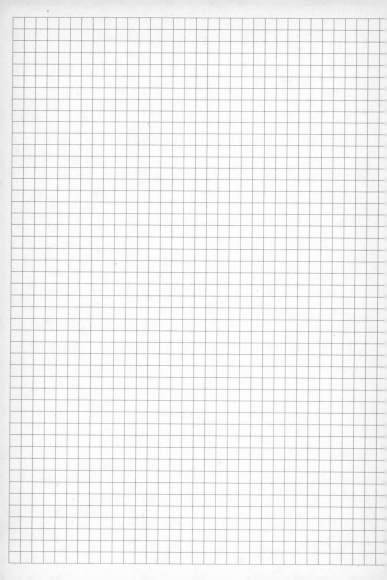

RESOURCES
ADDRESSES AND ROOM RATES

LANDMARKS

010 Moderna Museet
Skeppsholmen
T 5195 5200
www.modernamuseet.se

012 Kulturhuset
Sergels Torg 3
T 5083 1508
www.kulturhuset.
stockholm.se

012 Riksbanken
Brunkebergstorg 11
www.riksbank.com

013 Kaknästornet
Mörka Kroken 28-30
T 667 2105
www.kaknastornet.se

014 Koppartälten
Hagaparken
Solna
T 277 002
www.koppartalten.se

HOTELS

016 Hotel Rival
Room rates:
double, SEK1,390
Mariatorget 3
T 5457 8900
www.rival.se

017 Hotel Birger Jarl
Room rates:
double, SEK2,100;
Room 701, SEK2,500;
Room 705, SEK3,050;
Room 708, SEK3050;
Room 709, SEK2500;
Suite 710, SEK5,000
Tulegatan 8
T 674 1800
www.birgerjarl.se

018 Hotel Esplanade
Room rates:
double, SEK1,595;
Room 10, SEK1,695-
SEK2,995
Strandvägen 7a
T 663 0740
www.hotelesplanade.se

020 Berns Hotel
Room rates:
double, SEK2,600;
Rooms 606
and 608, SEK4,250;
Clock Suite, SEK8,500
Näckströmsgatan 8
T 5663 2200
www.berns.se

022 Nordic Light Hotel
Room rates:
double, SEK1,940;
Superior Mood
Suite, SEK2,990;
Deluxe Mood
Suite, SEK3,490;
Deluxe Corner
Room, SEK4,090
Vasaplan 7
T 5056 3000
www.nordiclighthotel.se

023 Grand Hôtel
Room rates:
double, SEK3,100;
Junior Suite, SEK6,500;
Bernadotte Suite,
SEK16,800
Södra Blasieholmshamnen 8
T 679 3500
www.grandhotel.se

026 Clarion Hotel
Room rates:
double, SEK1,700;
Söder Suite, SEK12,995;
Penthouse Suite, SEK5,000
Ringvägen 98
T 462 1000
www.clarion
stockholm.com

028 J Sealodge Gåshaga
Room rates:
double, SEK1,995
Värdshusvägen 14-16
Lidingö
T 601 3410
www.restaurantj.com

030 Hotel Hellsten
Room rates:
double, SEK1,690;
Suite 1201, SEK2,190;
Room 1302, SEK1,302
Luntmakargatan 68
T 661 8600
www.hellsten.se

24 HOURS

033 Lisa På Udden
Biskopsvägen 7
T 660 9475

034 Riddarbageriet
Riddargatan 15
T 660 3375

037 Kaffekoppen
Stortorget 20
T 203 170

037 Nobel Museum
Börshuset
Stortorget
T 5348 1800
www.nobel.org/nobel/
nobelmuseum

038 Bakfickan
Jakobs Torg 12
Operahuset
Kungsträdgarden
T 676 5809
039 Nox
Grev Turegatan 30
T 5458 2400
www.nox.se

URBAN LIFE
041 Grill
Drottninggatan 89
T 314 530
www.grill.se
042 Viola
Humlegårdsgatan 14
T 664 5535
www.sthlmsfinest.se
044 Edsbacka Krog
Sollentunavägen 220
T 963 300
www.edsbackakrog.se
045 Esperanto
Kunstensgatan 2
T 696 2323
www.esperanto
restaurant.se
046 Allmänna
Galleriet 925
Kronobergsgatan 37
T 4106 8100
www.ag925.se
048 Locanda Klara Norra
Mäster Samuelsgatan 60
T 440 2380
www.locanda.se

049 Teatergrillen
Nybrogatan 3
T 5450 3565
www.teatergrillen.se
050 Marie Laveau
Hornsgatan 66
T 668 8500
www.marielaveau.se
052 Fredsgatan 12
Fredsgatan 12
T 248 052
www.f12.se
053 Lux
Primusgatan 116
T 619 0190
www.luxstockholm.com
054 Haga Forum
Annerovägen 4
Solna
T 334 844
http://hagaforum.
gastrogate.com
056 Lilla Baren at Riche
Birger Jarlsgatan 4
T 5450 3560
www.riche.se
058 Operakällaren
Operahuset
Karl XII:s Torg
T 676 5801
www.operakallaren.se
059 The White Room
Regeringsgatan 61
T 5450 7665
www.whiteroom.se
060 Centro
Regeringsgatan 66
T 233 400
www.centro.nu

062 C/O Stockholm
Götgatan 30
T 5052 5951
www.costockholm.se
062 Deco Design
Odengatan 80
T 314 404
www.decodesignshop.com
062 Divino
Karlavägen 28
T 611 0269
062 Mrs H
Birger Jarlsgatan 9/
Smålandsgatan 10
T 678 0200
www.mrsh.se
062 Nitty Gritty
Krukmakargatan 26
T 240 044
www.nittygritty.se
062 Roppongi
Hantverkargatan 76c
T 650 1772
www.roppongi.se
062 Sabai-Soong
Linnégatan 39b
T 663 1277
062 Saturnus Café
Erikbergsgatan 6
T 611 7700
062 Skin Deep
Humlegårdsgatan 5
T 662 8270
062 Whyred
Norrlandsgatan 21
T 660 0170
www.whyred.se

ARCHITOUR

065 Stadsbiblioteket
Sveavägen 73
T 5083 1100
www.ssb.stockholm.se

068 Gåshaga Brygga
Gåshaga Brygga 13
T 282 828
www.boende.ncc.se

069 Millesgården
Herserudsvägen 32
Lidingö
T 446 7580
www.millesgarden.se

070 Södra Länken
Between Essingeleden
and Värmdöleden

SHOPPING

072 Acne
Nybrogatan 57a
T 5557 9900
www.acne.se

**072 Fifth Avenue
Shoe Repair**
Bondegatan 46b
T 214 808
www.shoerepair.se

072 Filippa K
Götgatan 23
T 5569 8585
www.filippa-k.se

072 Mrs H
Birger Jarlsgatan 9
T 678 0200
www.mrsh.se

072 Riddargatan 12
Riddargatan 12
T 611 0837

073 Svenskt Tenn
Strandvägen 5
T 670 1600
www.svensttenn.se

074 Modernity
Sibyllegatan 31
T 208 025
www.modernity.se

076 Gamla Lampor
Nybrogatan 3
T 611 9035
www.gamlalampor.com

078 Asplund
Sibyllegatan 3
T 662 5284
www.asplund.org

080 Konsthantverket
Södermalmstorg 4
T 611 0370
www.konsthantverkarna.se

**082 Orrefors/
Kosta Boda**
Birger Jarlsgatan 15
T 5450 4084
www.kostaboda.se

**083 10 Swedish
Designers**
Götgatan 25
T 643 2504
www.tiogruppen.com

084 Jacksons
Sibyllegatan 53
T 665 3350
www.jacksons.se

086 Apparat
Nytorgsgatan 36
T 653 6633
www.apparat.nu

SPORTS AND SPAS

088 Centralbadet
Drottninggatan 88
T 452 1300
www.centralbadet.se

**088 Kungliga
Tennishallen**
Lidingövägen 75
T 459 1500
www.kungltennishallen.com

089 Sturebadet
Sturegallerian 36
T 5450 1500
www.sturebadet.se

090 Globen Arena
Globentorget 2
T 771 310 000
www.globearenas.se

092 Yasuragi Spa
Hasseludden
Hamndalsvägen 6
Saltsjö-Boo
T 747 6100
www.yasuragi.se

094 Yacht Concept
Grand Hotel Saltsjöbaden
T 717 3650
www.yachtconcept.se

ESCAPES

WALLPAPER* CITY GUIDES

Editorial Director
Richard Cook

Art Director
Loran Stosskopf
City Editor
Alex Bagner
Project Editor
Rachael Moloney
Series Editor
Jeroen Bergmans
Executive Managing Editor
Jessica Firmin

Chief Designer
Ben Blossom
Designers
Sara Martin
Ingvild Sandal
Map Illustrator
Russell Bell

Photography Editor
Alicia Foley
Photography Assistant
Jasmine Labeau

Chief Sub-Editor
Jeremy Case
Sub-Editor
Clive Morris
Editorial Assistant
Felicity Cloake

Wallpaper* Group Editor-in-Chief
Jeremy Langmead
Creative Director
Tony Chambers
Publishing Director
Fiona Dent

Thanks to
Paul Barnes
Emma Blau
David McKendrick
Claudia Perin
Meirion Pritchard

PHAIDON

Phaidon Press Limited
Regent's Wharf
All Saints Street
London N1 9PA

Phaidon Press Inc
180 Varick Street
New York, NY 10014
www.phaidon.com

First published 2006
© 2006 Phaidon
Press Limited

ISBN 0 7148 4690 2

A CIP Catalogue record
for this book is available
from the British Library.

All rights reserved.
No part of this publication
may be reproduced,
stored in a retrieval system
or transmitted, in any
form or by any means,
electronic, mechanical,
photocopying, recording
or otherwise, without
the prior permission of
Phaidon Press.

All prices are correct at
time of going to press,
but are subject to change.

Printed in China

PHOTOGRAPHERS

Johan Fowelin
Moderna Museet,
pp010-011

Konsthantverket,
pp080-081
Apparat, p086

Peter Guenzel
Kulturhuset, p012
Koppartälten, pp014-015
Grill, p041
Viola, pp042-043
Edsbacka Krog, p044
Allmänna Galleriet 925,
pp046-047
Viktoria Hamberger, p063
Stadsbiblioteket,
pp066-067
Södra Länken, pp070-071
Gamla Lampor, pp076-077
Asplund, p078
Jacksons, pp084-085
Sturebadet, p089

Marianne Boströ
Kaknästornet, p013

Gabriella Wachtmeister
Stockholm City View,
inside front cover
Berns Hotel, pp020-021
J Sealodge Gåshaga,
pp028-029
Riddarbageriet,
pp034-035
Esperanto, p045
Locanda Klara Norra, p048
Marie Laveau, pp050-051
Haga Forum, pp054-055
Centro, pp060-061

Henrik Trygg
Djurgården, p033

Leila Latchin
Kaffekoppen, p037

Michael McLain
Teatergrillen, p049
Lilla Baren at Riche,
pp056-057

Max Plunger
Bakfickan, p038

Michael Rasche, Artur
Stadsbiblioteket, p065

Jason Tozer
Svenskt Tenn, p073
Schnapps, p079
10 Swedish
Designers, p083
Grebbestads Ansjovis
Original, p087

Peter Marlow, Magnum
Yachting, pp094-095

Lars Sundh
Oaxen Skärgårdskrog,
pp100-101

STOCKHOLM

A COLOUR-CODED GUIDE TO THE CITY'S HOT 'HOODS

ÖSTERMALM
The chic part of Stockholm, with snazzy shopping and grand residences

SKEPPSHOLMEN
Museum Island has all the culture you could possibly need, from art to design

NORRMALM
The financial and business centre of the city with office blocks and lunch spots

SÖDERMALM
Slightly leftfield district, full of cutting-edge boutiques and boho cafés

VASASTADEN
Friendly, residential area with an emerging scene of neighbourhood eateries

GAMLA STAN
The Old Town is the tourist hub, all cobbled streets and famous buildings

KUNGSHOLMEN
Up-and-coming residential area with loft-dwellers and galleries moving in

DJURGÅRDEN
Urban garden encompassing the zoo, funfair, restaurants and several museums

For a full description of each neighbourhood,
including the places you really must not miss, see the Introduction